Trapped in My Own Mind

Dale Grisso

Southern Collegiate Press

Southern Collegiate Press

Trapped in My Own Mind

Copyright © 2012 by Dale Grisso

ISBN: 978-1-936912-61-2   Softcover

This book was printed in the United States of America.

To order additional copies of this book, contact:

Southern Collegiate Press
1-423-475-7308
www.southerncollegiatepress.com

Special Thanks

This book-project would not have been possible without my supportive family, faithful friends, and the amazing students and faculty at Chattanooga State Community College.

So I want to say a special THANK YOU to those who contributed their support, expertise, and even personal input:

The Student Government Association
at Chattanooga State
... for offering your personal stories and sponsorship

Robin Popp, M.A. - Psychology Professor,
Chattanooga State
... for adding your powerful forward and expertise

Rachel Falu, M.S.Ed. - Instructor of English,
Chattanooga State
... for your critical guidance in the editing of this project

Great-aunt Millie & Grandma Iva - Joplin Tornado Survivors
Second-cousins Luke & Jana - Joplin Tornado Survivors
Uncle Phil & Aunt Barb - Joplin Tornado Survivors
Rita Barbery - Harrison Tornado Survivor
Isaac Craft - Original Cover Design

*Dedicated to all who are open
to analyze challenges,
and to those who courageously
tell their stories.*

Table of Contents

The Story Writing Itself

An invisible world holds more subjects than prisons,
With more gruesome tales than all man's dominions.

Few are able to tell of escape,
And those who do are too few and too late.

The sinister plot? To reign from within;
Mind and emotions kept in bondage grim.

Stories are told of challenging all sanity,
Smiles hiding the struggles of humanity.

To seek help they are afraid,
Bearing burdens alone and not for them made.

Life bringing its pain to women and men,
But ultimate trials coming deep from within.

They cry, 'What is the way out of this place?'
As keys escape them of freedom and grace.

But is this the end of their struggles here?
Or in search of the truth will their VICTORY appear?

Foreword

Trapped in My Own Mind is about us--- who we are and who we can become. The authors could be any one of us— all of us who know hurt and darkness. These personal experiences reflect our humanity---our pain, our struggles, our values, and our beliefs. The stories are about our habits that finally hurt so much that we are desperate enough to change our behaviors.

Although life holds few certainties, two things are certain: change and choice. We can choose to give-up or to grow towards our best selves. Choosing to walk through the fire of change does burn, and along the path there are many places to stumble and fall. But we can get up again and again. And each time the wounds heal more and we learn our strengths. We learn gratitude and compassion. We find our own truth.

To these stories of self-discovery, we can apply psychological perspectives. Humanistic psychology emphasizes free will, personal responsibility, and reaching our full potential. Self-awareness and self-acceptance are necessary but not always easy, since true self-examination reveals the good and the bad.

The author of the story *It's a Gift* expresses this well. "The fastest way to happiness is learning to accept who I am, gifts, flaws and all; and learning to love that person in the here and now, as I am today. Not who I may be, or who I was, but who I am."

The field of positive psychology also focuses on optimal human functioning. We can work with our virtues and skills to nourish positive emotions, traits, and relationships. No matter how low we feel, we can find something worthwhile in ourselves, and shift our momentum toward more uplifting experiences.

In chapter six, Stealth Deceit, the author writes, "I do not believe that influences and challenges in my life are actually the direct causes of depression. But the thoughts and emotional *reactions* that develop in me are what allow depression to take hold of me."

And in chapter four he states, "A lot of my struggles have not necessarily come from facts, but from what I *thought* was fact." These insights clearly reflect a principle of cognitive psychology; our negative thoughts may cause an emotional over-reaction. When we challenge our faulty thinking and replace it with more productive thinking, we activate the cycle of better thinking, better feeling, and better doing.

Once when I was down with bad times a friend simply said, "It is all part of it." I understood her reality check to mean that being human has its ups and downs and we don't just get the good times.

However, we do have some choice. We can suffer in self-recrimination and blame, or we can face our challenges and take responsibility for our healing and growth. We start our journey and find the journey fuels us forward. I wish you fulfilling travels.

Robin Popp, M.A.
Associate Professor of Psychology
Chattanooga State Community College

Preface

Alone. Helpless. Trapped. That is how I feel when waves of depression and negative feelings come over me. There seems to be no answers, and in the most intense moments, *no one* available to help.

Do you ever feel like you are drowning in life, but that you cannot let the people in your life know about it? That is me when I feel *trapped in my own mind.* It is as if no one could understand my thoughts, and as if telling them would just complicate things that much more. I then find myself living one life in front of people, but another life that only I know about.

Unfortunately, it took flirting with my own safety to realize how far I had progressed. One feeling had led to another. I finally realized that I was about to become one of those horrible stories people talk about. Or I could try to overcome, and use my story to help others.

Opening up is one of the hardest things I have ever done. I never wanted anyone to know about my struggles! But it also was the best first step I could have taken.

I decided to actually write out the frustrations going on inside me. There had to be someone else out there who also felt trapped. So maybe I could just relate to them. But I had no idea where this journey would actually take me.

For the first time, I experienced *release!* I also heard powerful stories from others. But this was just the beginning. Personal answers and resources came to light, and this project is the result. A negative spiral was truly turned into a positive ascent, and I hope you will join in this discovery of freedom!

Dealing with Depression

My Story

My story began with a little drama as a child, and a lot of negative thinking for years afterward. From childhood insecurities, to questioning my own value, I found a progression of feelings that went from anxiety, to rejection, to doubt, to planning how I would end it all. It's not what I wanted, but then again, it seemed for the best.

"The world doesn't need me...I am just a burden to others, and someone else will do my job better than I can. I've done as much as I'll ever do...It's time for me to go."

I became more and more miserable. I would cry my eyes out while driving down the road, to the point of not being able to see or hold the steering wheel. My head felt sometimes like it was about to explode, as the pressures of my own thoughts and feelings built up. I didn't want to pass this on to any future children, and I didn't want anyone to know what was really going on inside me either.

I picked a music score that was the tone of exactly how I felt. I also found a movie clip that I could loop on my tv, where the character says it's time for him to pass on. Somehow a picture also showed up, of myself waving "goodbye," seemingly to the world - in a weird sepia color. I have no idea who took the picture, when, or how it got to me (but I still have it).

So all this would be in the living room, as I lay lifeless on the couch. The picture and a note would be on the coffee table, addressed to my family and the world, explaining why this was best for everyone. I would apologize for all my failures, and state who I had truly loved.

I didn't know if I had the guts to slit my wrists, and I didn't want a mess for someone else to have to deal with.... But I had slit my own soul, and I believed I could literally 'will' my heart to give out. And if not, I certainly didn't have to turn the steering wheel that last time. Everything would be set up at home for others to find, and then it would all be over.

However, everything turned around when I decided to write out my personal story. The idea seemed *impossible* to do at first, because I didn't know exactly what I was dealing with. But I would try to find out. I had NO answers whatsoever. I only had a title, *Trapped In My Own Mind*, because that is exactly how I felt. I simply hoped that it would relate to someone else who might be feeling the same way.

But it actually gave me a reason to open up and talk about my struggles for the first time. Then I began discovering things about myself, which led to identifying the lies that were tearing me apart and leading me down a path of destruction. **I had to get to the *source* of what gets to me.**

From talking to my closest friends, professional counselors, and even celebrities, I've found secret struggles all around. For me, whether it was anxiety, anger, doubt, feelings of worthlessness, or even suicidal ideation, it came down to what I'm finding in common with so many others: *a habit of negative thinking.*

I believe we all have *something* that gets to us. And while we hide our weaknesses, we may also be hiding our own **value and potential**, even from *ourselves*. And yes, I have to repeat the process when they try to return. But when I identified the triggers that were setting off my depressive feelings, their power over me was broken.

I know that the story of our life can be made out of different situations for each of us, and require different resources to help. *Please seek those resources!* But I also know that we can choose from this point to hold a pen in that story. And all in all, *each of us can have our own story to tell!*

Introduction

Someone recently told me that depression almost *destroyed* them this past year. As I began talking with my friends about my struggles, they also opened up with stories of their own.

The Center for Disease Control reported on March 31, 2011, that an estimated 1 in 10 American adults are affected by depression (http://www.cdc.gov). I also did an online search using the words "celebrities and depression," and was blown away by the results. Why are negative feelings so widespread, so deep and powerful, drowning people seemingly at will? And why me?

There was a battle going on inside myself... thoughts that questioned my present value and future potential. I had a job I enjoyed, supportive parents, and awesome friends at college and church. So why was I struggling at all?

Finally one day at a concert, with tears in my eyes, I knew something had to give. I felt trapped inside my own mind, believing I couldn't tell anybody, but not able to get the answers to my struggles either. It seemed impossible to analyze what had been plaguing me for years now.

I decided to write out my story, challenging the thoughts that had been challenging me. I looked for the ideas that questioned my value, and questioned *them.* Was there a REAL basis to feeling I had no personal worth or future potential? I started seeking proof of my value, which seemed impossible to do while battling negative thoughts. But I had to begin telling myself the *facts*, not buying into hopeless ideas about myself.

Then one night the realization came to me that some of my ideas, and even some feelings, **were just LIES.** At that moment a huge weight lifted off me. I also began to realize that I had developed a **"habit of negative thinking."** But now I could begin identifying my vulnerabilities, watching out for the specific ideas and feelings that get to me, and get me down.

But with this also came the discovery that others, including friends closest to me, were describing the same feelings I had. Normal, smart and even successful people, related to my issues, as well as having many other challenges. I was NOT ALONE.

Through this I made one of the best discoveries of all: I was not weird or crazy! The more I talked to people, the more I found that we all have hidden struggles and weaknesses. WE ARE HUMAN! I would not just be thrown out by everyone as "a mental health case." And I did not have to blindly follow empty pep talk or guesses in treatment. I just needed to find the appropriate behaviors and resources that truly worked for *me*.

I am not a mental health professional, and some struggles need professional treatment. **So if there is a chance you are facing clinical depression or other disorders, please seek appropriate resources without delay.** At least start by seeking advice or counseling from someone you trust. Resources are more available than ever before, so please don't forfeit any more of your life to problems that could actually be dealt with.

While driving my car around a curve, I debated not turning the wheel, letting the road just end it all. But now I've found a purpose, as daily struggles become opportunities for growth and outreach. We all have a story to tell, and are *not really defeated unless we give up*. So let's overcome instead of being overcome, and BE that positive story of freedom!

Harrison, TN – March 2nd, 2012

This piece of wood was blasted through Rita Barbery's home by the Harrison tornado, completely embedded in the external wall.

It lodged in her vanity mirror, pointing at her bed. After taking this picture, while helping with clean-up at Rita's home, I was reminded of the piercings from negative experiences in so many of our lives. Worse yet, our internal "mirror" may be shattered as well, reflecting a broken view of ourselves.

Invisible Threats

Secret Insecurities

*"What if I'm the only person dealing with this?
And if I talk, what if no one understands me?"*

W ho expected beautiful weather in Joplin to turn into a historic tornadic storm that fateful day of May 22nd, 2011? Less than thirty minutes before impact, Joplin received warning of a monster tornado that took four homes from my relatives. In minutes, thousands of lives were changed forever.

I stay glued to the weather during tornado and hurricane seasons, as storms literally seem to appear out of nowhere on radar. Meteorologists say it only takes a few key ingredients to produce disastrous weather conditions. And such warnings have turned out to be matters of life and death for many.

But many of us are facing another storm brewing within. "Little" clouds of negative *thoughts and feelings* escape our internal radar, yet are the right ingredients for a personally disastrous storm.

Have you ever known someone who looked happy on the outside, but revealed a completely different attitude underneath their smile? Perhaps we've all BEEN that person.

Even some of the most prominent people in society have hidden *insecurities*, powerful *oppression*, internal *depression*, and even *hostilities* brewing within.

Some take out their frustrations on the things around them, and even hurt others. But some are "bottlers," holding their frustrations *in*, hurting themselves. I am a bottler.

And yes, life brought unexpected challenges. But the invisible progression of negative thoughts was the biggest challenge for me, and I woke up in a self-destructive downward spiral.

So how did I go from being a happy person, to considering if I should end it all? Shouldn't my mind and emotions be in my control? Why then had my personal radar been on "stand-by"?

Time Traveling
I began wondering where it all started. And then an opportunity came to find out. One weekend my second-cousin and I decided to meet at the property where we used to play as kids. This place took me back to some stressful memories, (unknown to her), and I took off to the physical locations where those memories had been made.

Emotions came flooding back as I chose to stand in the *exact* spots where all those things had happened. It was as if I had literally time-travelled to my past. I could see everyone in my mind, hearing what they were saying all over again.

Things were about to explode. Everyone was tense, and some words had already been said that didn't need to be said. Even more would take place in private than in public.

But the whole situation felt like it would blow at any minute. And I was caught in the middle. Calls for my loyalty pulled me apart from all sides. Fear grew exponentially.

My head began to burn. Circumstances were out of my control, and since they involved everyone around me, I was left with no one to talk to. Worse yet, I didn't know how to personally respond to the immense pressures building up inside me.

Where Did It All Start?

Our family was different, and we felt what it was like to be down, and to be kicked while down. We didn't fit in, and were looked on as "lower class" by some.

Finances and religion were our family's biggest stigmas. And as with cliques, gang-violence, and bullying, it came down to feeling stereotyped, socially abused, and even exiled by others. Worse yet, I carried things alone as a child, beginning to blame myself, as if circumstances were somehow my fault. *Would everyone look at me like this for the rest of my life?*

My security was naturally tied to my parents. But when times got tough, they struggled as well, and that security was eroded. Confidence in myself wasn't developed enough to adjust to these new challenges. Fear of these things made me feel even smaller. I really believe this was the first step to later questioning my own self-value.

As a child I did not even know the term "insecurity," so I didn't know how to identify the different feelings within me. I also didn't know how to tell my parents or anyone else what I was dealing with. Circumstances seemed much bigger than me, bigger than life, and of course, *bigger than they actually were.*

Even now when I don't believe I can handle something, insecurities become crippling. They can practically stop whatever I am trying to do. For example, when I am playing the piano in public, I can feel the strength literally leave my hands.

Whether as a child or an adult, insecurities brought a strange paralysis that could affect my whole life. And age had not guaranteed maturity. So could I still be subconsciously living in my childhood in some areas of my life?

I Can Handle It . . .

As I grew older and situations changed, I buried the feelings of childhood insecurity. But bigger struggles began to develop, progressing slowly, innocently, almost invisibly at first. But once the gate of insecurity was opened, other pressures were also able to get in. For example, the perfectionist in me was starting to come out, and I became my own worst critic.

I was the oldest of three, the independent one, keeping to myself. Introversion also runs in our family, and because I was so quiet, Mom would sometimes ask if I was ok. I always said that I was. I liked my space, and didn't want issues to become any bigger than they had to be. I even kept physical pain to myself. Involving others was a last resort.

I don't understand why, but it is still extremely hard for me to tell people I am struggling with anything. *"They might misunderstand or misjudge."* I always think I have to struggle alone. *"I can figure it out."* But it usually gets worse.

Even in adulthood my response to new challenges was to return to childhood insecurities, such as fear, tension, and self-blame.

A Personal Confrontation

Back at the old property, my second cousin and I ended up in the living room, after I had privately relived all those intense childhood memories. Each of us was just sitting quietly. All of a sudden she began to ask me how that old house made me feel. She later told me that she didn't know why she asked that question. But it penetrated a hidden area of my life. And that made me very uncomfortable. She was family, and one of my best friends. But I didn't have to tell her anything, right? I had *never* told anyone about those feelings before, and refused to give away any answers in my facial expressions.

So I blew off her question with the smoothest answer I could think of... that good ole standby, "*I feel mixed emotions.*" But she was surprised, not expecting an answer like that. This prompted more "nosey" questions from her.

She wanted to know what I meant by "mixed emotions." But what would she think if I told her the truth? This was extremely personal, involving our whole family. Plus, I didn't want to depress her with my negative memories and warped childhood views of reality. Aren't we supposed to just be positive?

But her questions were hard to dodge, and as I began to open up, I watched her face to see how she would respond. I'd go silent the second she looked judgmental. But she didn't flinch, so I decided to take one of the biggest leaps I have ever taken with anyone, and just tell her my experiences, and how they had really made me feel.

Years of pent-up feelings and childhood thoughts were coming out for the first time. And something was happening that I did not see coming. I began to feel *free* – ironically, on the very property where all those struggles had started!

It was a moment of fate. Bottled-up pressures were now being brought out and identified. I also began to analyze how small they actually were, confronting them with my adult mind. I realized that I no longer had to see life through the eyes of my childhood insecurities.

As I became alive with answers to my past, a verse also played in my mind. *"All things work together for good to those who love God.. "* (Romans 8:28). It was a moment of truth that I will never forget. The past has an answer. The present has strength. And the future really does have hope.

I cannot always run from my problems, just like I couldn't run from childhood situations. But I cannot blame everything on my past either, even though tempted at times to give up on people, and even life itself.

I decided to walk the old property one more time before we left. And yes, I relived the same memories again. But this time I was smiling on the inside. I had a new perspective, not based on fear and insecurities, but on finding **wisdom for situations** (before I respond negatively), **confidence in myself** (to handle anything given me), **and faith in God** (over the things I cannot control.) I will never forget the peace (John 14:24-27) I felt.

I left that old place a different person. And I have a long way to go. But I will forever be grateful to Sara-Ruth for walking me through my past, and not judging, but supporting me to my first taste of freedom from childhood insecurities.

Identify, Familiarize, Take Action!

Identify what you're going through. Stressing just complicates things and doesn't deal with the actual problem at all. But knowing what you're dealing with can be half the battle to overcoming it.

Familiarize yourself with what you are dealing with, its causes, and how you're reacting. Try to eliminate the element of surprise. Talk to those who may understand. And if you find yourself in a negative progression, learn where you are and why you are feeling low, so you can respond.

Take action! Address those internal challenges with positive facts. Consider seeking outside resources. Also consider the GIFT in your story. A negative situation could be your opportunity to find unique growth and purpose. You may be the only person someone else will relate to. And you may become the only one who will keep that person alive.

Joplin, MO – May 22nd, 2011

My Uncle Phil hid in a closet behind the center wall, as my Aunt Barb looked up to see the roof fly away. They were both spared by inches, as winds took their Joplin home apart.

As I drove through Joplin and visited each of the destroyed homes of my relatives, I pictured what I believe is happening to many on the inside. The winds of fear and anxiety tear through our lives, ripping off the roof of our security, exposing our internal vulnerabilities.

Silent Struggles

A Monster Named Anxiety

*"True deliverance is not running,
but overcoming."*

The Worst Conspiracy Theory

When we were young, my two siblings and I had different school experiences, including public, private, and home schooling. We also loved athletics. But our family could not afford organized community teams. Therefore, street soccer and softball became staples of our social life.

As a teenager, however, I began spending a lot of time by myself, just sitting in my room and trying to figure things out. It was then that new insecurities about life emerged. Earlier childhood stress had been caused by external circumstances, but this was different. It was *internal*, in my thoughts.

"What if" questions began to surface about everything around me. *"What if I really couldn't trust anything? What if I messed up, playing right into the hands of evil?"*

These thoughts sounded extreme, but also seemed impossible for me to answer as a teenager. And as I questioned, the reality around me was being reinvented subconsciously. I couldn't come to grips with these fears, so the lines of reality were blurred. Yes indeed I was playing into an evil hand – not of the dark forces of evil, but of *fear itself.* This was also drawing me into my own world that much more.

I was afraid to step outside the box I had created, which became crippling to my daily life. I began to feel anxiety, which ended up setting in and tormenting me literally non-stop as I sought answers. I was now staying in my room constantly, only coming out if I had to. But I also began to seek excuses to come out, because being around others actually helped, though I wouldn't talk to them about what I was thinking.

Wasn't all this just in my head? Yes, most likely, I thought. But wait, did that mean I was going crazy? No, because at least I knew better. But I felt like I would go crazy if this continued.

I didn't think anyone had the answers, so I slowly squeezed my family and friends out of my daily life. And since I wasn't talking out my feelings, insecurity and fears had free reign. I thought that if I asked certain questions about life, I might be branded as crazy. I also *never* dreamed of publishing these things. But **personal openness is KEY,** no matter the struggle.

I knew struggles were taking down my whole morale, as I secretly begged for answers. But I absolutely couldn't find them, and didn't know what else to do. *"What if"* questions had taken over, and I became a really frustrated 16-year old.

Basic activities like eating and studying were kept up, giving the impression that things were normal. But my parents knew I was quieter, and tried to ask about it. I didn't give an answer.

Talking to someone would have made me vulnerable, I felt. Plus it would have been embarrassing, especially since I was questioning everything.

If I had tried talking out my questions, perhaps I would have received the answers I needed. *Answers were actually all around me for the taking, but I was afraid to just get out there where they were.*

My bedroom was my haven, my private fortress, where I stayed almost ALL the time now. But it actually had become my personal prison, where I was 'frozen in place,' literally. I spent nine months in almost absolute silence.

Stress became unbearable, as fears turned my life into a pressure-cooker. My bedroom was in the back of the house, and one day I made sure I was alone, when no one would come back there. I had to deal with the pressure, but definitely not in front of anyone else.

I let the stress build. Things got so intense that I held onto my chair with a vice-grip, lifting myself off the seat. My brain felt like it was about to crack. I wasn't sure what the technical definition of "nervous breakdown" was, but I knew it was imminent, because I was quickly coming to the end of what I could handle. If you've been there, you know what I mean.

The moment froze, and in a mental flash I did an intellectual vital-signs checkup. I still had logical thoughts and knew my brain was intact. I had strength but my nerves were about to give. I also had mental control, because it was my own thoughts that had worked me up. But fear was real too, and the worst fear was of being trapped in this lifestyle forever.

I could feel myself falling, and knew I was about to hit rock-bottom. The bottom actually seemed to be flying up towards me. I was an internal free-fall.

Then all of a sudden it was as if a supportive Hand came under me. My nervousness just *stopped.* I wasn't going to crash. I hadn't figured it all out yet, but I could make it. "The eternal God is thy refuge, and underneath are the everlasting arms." (Deuteronomy 33:27) I will never forget that feeling.

Why the fear? It was my response to insecurities and questions about life. Others might respond by acting out in extreme ways. Even whole societies have been driven by phobias, which created some of our saddest moments in history. But I learned that fear can be just as devastating *on the inside.* **Fear is not a solution; just a negative** *response* **to the problem.**

A Personal Technique for Dealing with Anxiety

Months had now gone by since that most intense moment of almost cracking. But the struggles had not gone away. I was still dealing with the same intense anxiety every day. But I will never forget the exact moment when I saw through my fear.

This particular evening I had been in a continuous struggle like every other evening, and I was forcing myself to get ready for bed. But as I jumped in the shower, there was something magical about the water. I think the relaxing effect got to me, because all of a sudden I became bold.

I decided to get on the "other side" of my mental journey of fear. I looked at the last nine months of my life *in third person,* as if I was trying to help a friend. Somehow this automatically put me on top of my struggles. I could see them *objectively.*

Then it hit me... it didn't matter what the "what if" questions were about. The *root* issue was the *fear itself*. Even if I couldn't answer all my questions, I still could work on the emotional response to my questioning. **I realized that overreacting to "problems" was actually *creating* problems!**

The mental 'spell' was broken. Anxiety had been present so long that it had become a lifestyle. But when I was able to *separate emotions from real problems*, it all clicked. And more challenges were still to come, of course! But I now had a vital realization in my journey.

I also learned that we can be limited in our life *without* a physical handicap. Anxiety can limit us almost at will, and without being based on facts. And sometimes we feel trapped, but we must break the cycle of giving in to our fears and believing that we are trapped.

If you relate to these experiences, and cannot find answers in a reasonable amount of time, please talk to someone about it! Get an objective opinion about things that are bothering you. Don't go for weeks or months like I did, stressing out, with no improvement. I thought I HAD to handle things by myself. But answers were available the whole time.

Why was Faith not the Answer?

I grew up in a religious home, and had even found a strong personal faith as a child. The Bible became a daily discovery of lessons that changed my life, and actually worked! But spirituality did not make me immune to my own fears, or any other personal challenges. And regardless of what some teach, not all challenges are "sin," and outside resources really are sometimes needed.

But when my emotions were intense, it seemed like faith, or what I thought was part of my faith, was actually *complicating* things. And yes I "prayed" and sought a Divine answer from the Bible, but got absolutely *nothing.* It seemed to be actually making things worse! Where were the answers all of a sudden?

An important lesson had to come to light for me. Some fears had been created BY me, and the answers were to come the same way. So in these moments it was actually Divine *silence* which was speaking the loudest. I had to take a look at ME.

I was learning to combine *fortitude in myself* with faith. I had to step up and use my own mind, strength and confidence. When I did this, everything, including my spiritual life, was back on track. Religion for me could not just be about floating through life on a magical carpet of belief. I too had to live.

What Pushes Your Buttons?

Continual experiences with anxiety led to being alone, frustrated, and later down the road, depressed. But the progression was subtle, starting with certain situations or "buttons" that could get it to me. These were sometimes "small" or "silly" things.

For example, when my car would break down on the side of the interstate (which has happened a *few* times), then a volcano of fear would swell in me. Immediately I would think things like, *"You are stuck; this will NEVER be fixed; you will fail in your responsibilities, and your whole life will be over... ."*

If I didn't catch these thoughts early, they would quickly turn into emotion. I'd begin cringing, sweating and talking to myself desperately. (I now have a cell phone and travelers' insurance).

But my bigger "buttons" have to do with fear that I don't measure up in life. Maybe I am behind! Perhaps I am not where others are, or where I should be, at my age. And now as a young adult, it seems everyone but me has a family, nice house, "status-symbol" car and name brand clothes, etc. But though I'm working on it, I'm nowhere near that status in life.

Then we see success stories in the media, and it drives the point home even deeper. I begin judging my own value by comparing myself to others. Perhaps in all the commercials and celebrity lifestyles thrown at us, **we lose sight of our own value and how to be secure in who we already are.**

For me, identity-anxiety spelled out in three ways: 1. *Fear* of not keeping up with the identity that others have. 2. *Fear* of not fitting in. 3. *Fear* that I am behind and can't move forward in life like everyone else. These thoughts became the fuel for my later depression.

Occasionally I take time to stop and identify every "button" I can think of that gets me down. I look at what got me down during the day, or in the past week. I then try to take note of these areas so they don't catch me off guard the next time.

I made a unique discovery though. Not all of my "buttons" originated with me. Some are clearly hereditary, being the same weaknesses seen in generations before me. In knowing my relatives and where I come from, I am actually getting to know MYSELF better. Then I can watch for those "genetic buttons," having more control over what pushes them.

I do not blame everything on genetics, and I am thankful for the many good qualities that have been passed down.

But I also believe we are made up of choices, and that no one is bound to a negative identity, regardless of family history. **Who we are can be weakened or strengthened, depending on our focus, and who we want to become.**

People Issues
Another source of anxiety for me has been social situations. And please note that they ARE going to come, no matter how agreeable or nice we are. But I hate conflict! When something seems to go wrong socially, I always imagine the worst. Many days and sleepless nights have been spent worrying if someone was offended or at odds with me.

If I have failed socially, it will haunt my thoughts for the rest of the week, and even stay with me for months or years. Some things I have still not gotten over, such as a sharp word spoken out of frustration. **Most situations are not nearly as bad as I imagine,** but I usually don't see this until well after I have worried about them non-stop.

I have discovered that if I think there is a problem, offering a simple apology can bring personal peace. I can then rest and be confident that I've done my part. This may also open the door to a better relationship with those whom we offended.

Romance and Relationships
One of my most stressful and emotional anxieties was regarding romance. I would wrestle with feelings for someone, then try to figure out their feelings for me. But I would be too afraid to actually ask, leaving me to "stew" indefinitely.

Then the stress of thinking I was missing out on a possible relationship would build up until I felt sick, as I blamed myself for not having done enough. I would pressure myself about it until my head literally felt on fire from the inside. One Valentine's night I wanted to ask a girl out, but ended up stressing so much about it that I felt sick, lying on the floor.

Obviously I had to learn a better way of dealing with situations, rather than just stressing over them. Some tips have included taking a realistic look at the whole situation (minus my emotions), and even asking a friend what they know.

Then I consider making the phone call to just casually ask someone where they are in dating. This opens the door to possibly finding out how they feel about me personally.

But most importantly, I discovered that my emotions, unchecked, (especially fear) would show me no mercy. We have to take control, accepting whatever the outcome is.

New Developments
As a teenager, anxiety also took another form. I became very self-conscious when I was placed outside my comfort zone. The simplest things, such as walking through the mall, were extremely painful experiences for me. I would feel like everyone was watching me, judging my every move, and wondering why I was even there in the first place.

I would look down and find something wrong with what I was wearing, which led me to imagine that others were also criticizing my appearance. I wouldn't be able to look anyone in the eye as I passed them. And unless I was with others, I felt like I had to get out of there immediately.

To add to this, I am very thin, which, believe it or not, plays a huge part in my personal confidence. For example, wearing a short-sleeved shirt gets to me, because it makes me feel skinnier in how I *think* I look to others.

Also, when I was on any team as a child, the teachers would line us up according to height. Guess who would be the last one in line every time? This was always embarrassing (but even though I was the smallest, I later discovered I could also be the fastest).

It took me a long time to discover that insecurities and fears are a part of being human. And if you mention them to someone who really listens, you will most likely be surprised to find that they have felt the same things. While each of us is unique, we also have much in common. This discovery can change our whole perspective.

A positive view of myself is one of the hardest things I dealt with, even daily. I didn't feel like I really had anything to offer. So many times I didn't pursue new things. I just didn't think I deserved them. I wouldn't even allow myself to think that way.

Finding Answers
Perhaps the worst of all fears is the fear of the unknown. As a young adult, one particular social situation had me in extreme anxiety, but I didn't tell my parents for a month.

Finally I went to my dad, and he reminded me of a similar situation I had dealt with in the past. In a moment of time I saw exactly what I was dealing with, and it gave me immediate relief. I realized that I just needed to accept them the way they were, instead of getting worked up about them.

This was the day that I discovered "*the power of familiarity.*" I realized that I had already dealt with this type of situation before. This also brought me to a more mature response.

But I've also had to learn when to stay in a situation and when to get away. There is a time to take a break, collecting ourselves and finding the right responses. Sometimes this is as simple as going to the restroom to get away for a minute. But some situations are so intense that they are not fixable as they are. And if we can't handle them, it's better to get away than to over-react and make a big issue bigger.

However, running from problems is rarely an option. So sometimes I make the mistake of ignoring them and delaying my response, hoping they will just go away. Better to "nip it in the bud."

But at some point when I've done all I can, I have to be confident to just accept things for what they are, finding the good in them, and knowing that all will work out for the best.

I want a *microwave life...* I want things fixed RIGHT AWAY! But even "unfixable" relationships or unavoidable losses can be survived. **And I found that sometimes problems contain a hidden message, leading us to something better, bringing the opportunity to start a new chapter in our lives.**

Joplin, MO – May 22nd, 2011

My great-aunt Millie stood alone on the steps between the basement and first floor, as EF-5 tornadic winds swirled around her house. The brick garage, chimney, and metal hand rails were literally "eaten" away.

Hamster Wheel

Seclusion & Loneliness

*"We might adjust to being alone,
but it's much harder adjusting to being lonely."*

The Hamster Wheel Turns

Outdoor walks have always been a way of escape for me. Nature gives me a place where I can think freely, as well as dream about my future. It has also been a place to withdraw and think through the things life brings me.

But I didn't realize that too many secluded moments eventually were leading me to longer-term isolation. I was getting drawn into my own world, where I never wanted to come out.

In my teen years our family made a big move to another state. And of course we didn't really know anyone there. My dad had gotten a new job, and my brother and sister moved seamlessly into new social circles.

But I will never forget the day when they all left the house to begin their week of designated activities. However, I had to stay home, bringing the deepest feeling of loneliness I had ever experienced.

This may not make sense to everyone, but for me there was a difference between being alone and being lonely. I loved being by myself, and it actually "reset" me for going into the world again.

But I don't think any of us want to be *lonely.* One we choose, the other chooses us. One was about where I was; the other was about how I felt. And I made the mistake of connecting that feeling with *who* I was. As I entered new situations later, that horrible feeling of loneliness returned, and I embarked on deeper journey of questioning my self-worth.

A New Kind of Pain
Loneliness *hurts.* Left to itself, I believe it becomes like a sickness, and is even the silent killer of many.

It's lonely at the top, and it's lonely in a crowd, but it's also lonely right *after* the crowd. There were times where I felt at the top of my social game. But when it was all over, and no one was left to talk to, then it felt as if no one cared. That hit me the hardest. I was ending up with no lasting friendships. There were times that I screamed on the inside for just *one* true friend.

Being around unfamiliar people made me lonelier. Hearing people talk, but having no one to talk to, is one of the worst situations I found myself in.

I learned to keep myself company, and personal journaling became my best friend. I spent all my free time planning and writing out the future. It was then that I discovered my love for media, particularly TV production, which led eventually to my major at college.

But though I kept myself occupied, the feeling of loneliness tempted me to question my own social value.

Feeling lonely is natural, but how we let it affect our perspective on life is another matter. This became a root cause of my future depression. *"Nobody will miss me."*

I did adjust to the pain that came with being alone, but I withdrew into my own world to do that. And even though I became comfortable, I was also becoming "trapped."

The Hamster Wheel Speeds Up

Though I finally made new acquaintances where we moved, soon our family was in for the shock of our lives. It was as if in one day EVERYTHING fell apart.

Social conflict came, and as a family we learned that it's one thing to be alone among many people, but it's another thing to be alone with many people *against* you. And there are not many things lonelier than losing your social status among your friends, becoming the "outcasts" of your own social network.

Misunderstandings were mostly the cause, and all of a sudden each member of our family felt attacked. It seemed everyone was after us. But we were all we had as a family, and we became each other's best friends. We finally had a special family relationship that I wouldn't trade for anything.

But though this loss strengthened our family, it did not help my personal loneliness. Rather, it drove me more into my own world, becoming another "nail in the coffin."

No "Exit" Sign in the Hamster Wheel

Adjusting to loneliness can help us cope, but it also has a great danger. It contains the hidden trap of the hamster wheel. We become occupied with running along in our own little world.

And when I developed this comfort zone for myself, I lost sight of the need for others in my life. I did not realize that I was not only missing out on potential friendships, but also on the perspective and value that others could add in my life.

But I didn't want anyone to pop the bubble. I could think what I wanted, and there was no one around to disagree with me. However, when times got tough, I didn't have anyone there to disagree with my negativity either, or support me.

I believe that over time, wanting to stay isolated from others can become an *addiction...* a dangerous hamster wheel that enslaves us from overcoming our challenges.

The Art of Making Friends
When I felt lonely, I assumed people were rejecting me. The hamster wheel became a fast track to depression for me.

Sometimes I am not really alone, I just *feel* lonely because I don't have someone to talk to at the moment. And it seems that when I am really fired up to chat, no one is available. But I have to learn to be flexible with people's availability.

And this brought out one of my greatest weaknesses: *taking things personal when they don't work out,* even to the point of emotional damage.

When I feel lonely, sometimes I have to just get out there and talk to someone. It proves to me psychologically that I can have friends again. Sometimes it's just a matter of finding the person with no one to talk to, and going for a conversation.

And instead of just staring at someone with nothing to say, I look for **casual conversation.** Then I find something **in common** to discuss, which takes away the awkward social pressure, and builds my confidence.

I also discovered the simple art of smiling. We can ALL show an expression of positivity to melt the ice, and it works. I found that **many people were just as scared to talk to me as I was to them!** Taking the initiative to be friendly has opened up all kinds of doors. *Somebody has to make the first move.*

One of the easiest ways I have come out of my shell is to make an observation about where I am, commenting on it to someone. Then I just see where it goes. If they don't really respond, it's no real loss, because it was just a rhetorical comment anyway. But people like to communicate and express opinions.

I also try to show enthusiasm about whom I'm talking to. *People seem to react the way we act toward them.* I try to find a reason to be motivated about talking to them, and about whatever I'm saying.

It's *contagious!* If I am motivated, it's more likely they will want to be around me. I try putting negative thoughts or other personal struggles aside, unless the person relates (which can then become one the greatest ways to connect to them).

I've since had to learn the difference between a true friend and an acquaintance. Connections may begin by relating, but they are maintained by sharing with each other *on a regular basis*. I have to consistently push myself to stay in communication.

Being a Friend to Someone

Many times we do not know what others are dealing with privately, though they may appear to be living a "normal" life. Sometimes these are the quiet people. I have *been* that person. But sometimes it only takes one magical moment of "bonding" to begin a lifelong friendship.

A calm silent person may actually have a LOT going on within them. That's why I am trying hard not to judge anyone by how they look, because there is so much more to them than meets the eye. It has been life-altering to step outside my comfort zone, and yes, even my sacred clique, to talk to new people.

Being friendly to others can make them feel valuable, just like we feel when someone talks to us. Your very attention could be the thing someone else is looking for. And it's a free gift we all can share!

I am also learning to be mindful of even my closest friends. Just because they are my best friend does not mean I know everything about them. They could really be dealing with something and just afraid to say it.

I also try to be open with my friends about my struggles, so that they can feel free to share too. I try not to over-do it or become annoying, and I always try to show myself as a non-critical listener. **Half of every conversation is just** *listening*. **And** *everyone* **needs a listener.**

I've met some people whom no one really listens to. And I believe things are bottling up in our whole society. This has put me on the quest of trying to be there for as many people as I can, because it could have made the difference in my life.

"Don't let people be your worst cause of loneliness, when they can be your greatest cure for loneliness!"

Joplin, MO – May 22nd, 2011

We never imagined that the mighty icons of my great-aunt's home would end up on their face. But neither did I imagine that doubts would one day erode my security in things I thought were without doubt.

Call to Reckoning

A Plague of Doubt

*"Doubts said that my reality was false and just based on emotions;
but I found that the DOUBTS were false
and were playing with my emotions."*

Intelligence?
For millennia, the human mind has been the source of creative intelligence. And after years of science fiction movies, technicians are finally claiming to engineer artificial intelligence that "computes" and makes decisions like we do every day.

However, our human creative abilities also have another side to them. Our intelligence can also "create" problems and doubts, along with other negative things. And so it has been for me. A lot of my struggles have not necessarily come from facts, but from what I *thought* was fact.

The Hard Questions About Lifestyle identity
As I exited my teen years, loneliness was not as big of a challenge to me, though it still re-surfaced occasionally (like in negative social situations, which will always come and go).

However, another change was taking place in my life, as I now began to think for myself in a whole new way. I began challenging my roots (including the way I was raised), and with this I discovered tunnels of doubt.

I began to challenge my identity, and who I really was. My religious views came first. And what about my religious family? Did I want to identify with them anymore, especially the things that seemed overly strict?

Spiritual things by default are invisible, having no physical evidence. They are also becoming more and more popular in society to question, whether in scientific discussion or otherwise.

So my young adult questions began. Were spiritual things just invented by mankind to give security and direction in life? Had I invented my own "God" that I could feel and that could "lead" me, but that was completely in my head? Could all my religious experiences simply be explained by subjective emotions?

And what about alternative lifestyles? Even close friends had announced different identities. Who was I? Was I different than what my birth certificate said? Would I need to make an announcement, even if it made my family uncomfortable? What would be the consequences? Would I become the rebel of the family? Would I be an outcast?

Any big changes in my identity would have been complicated. And those who come from a strong family or faith background know exactly what I mean. But what were my feelings telling me? I felt different at times, but was it just psychological, media-influenced, or even hormonal?

These thoughts became a huge struggle for me, not only spiritually and intellectually, but emotionally as well. A small crisis ensued in my heart of hearts, which I felt I could tell NO ONE about.

However, I didn't make any announcements. And I am so glad I waited, because even though I had different hormonal influences and tendencies, I was the same person I had been all along.

But it took time to sort all this out, and in the mean time I almost put a huge rift between myself and my family, as well as everything else I knew. And by the time I figured things out, it would have seemed impossible to go back.

The Debate

Have you ever had an argument in your mind? I felt I had evidence to prove different points than what I had believed. I then got so frustrated that I "debated" God on multiple topics, and each "debate" could last for weeks on end. These debates then began to really challenge my worldview.

But then I examined the *basis* for my worldview. A lot of beliefs come from religious writings. But what about them? Yes, reading the Bible had taught me good things, given me promises to claim, a purpose in life, and real change. But was it all really true in the first place?

What about seeming contradictions? What about statements that don't sound socially acceptable? And after all, just because a book claims it is from God doesn't make it so.

Answers didn't come to mind right away, and many times I would get very frustrated, seeing only the negative sides of an argument. This created an emotional struggle that went beyond the question of faith. My impression of life itself also began to waiver.

My stability in everything was shaken. I also condemned myself for doubting things in the first place. I felt like a hopelessly bad person. I began to act different around my family. I acted as if I was that "bad" person I had "become" for doubting.

But I also didn't want anyone to know I was questioning what I had always been taught, and had even been respected for. It felt like my foundation was eroding literally out from under me.

Light at the End of the Tunnel

I finally went privately to a friend (Rebekah Farnsworth) whom I had grown up with. She said others had been describing the same doubts to her, and we all had one thing in common: our AGE. *It was that time in life of coming to conclusions for ourselves.*

As soon as Rebekah said this, it clicked. I wasn't bad or crazy; I was becoming an adult and thinking for myself. This advice was critical and a timely blessing to me.

I realized that I had to look past my thoughts, to what I could see that really worked in my life. For example, even during the times that I doubted, I was still blessed, daily, in ways I couldn't explain. I decided to build my faith on the realities of truth in my life, not on tradition or the pride of holding on to what I had always been told.

Life came alive again for me, and my foundation was strengthened in a whole new way. I also discovered that questioning things was NOT wrong or unhealthy, but actually made me more grounded.

I also discovered that my deep doubting didn't originate from facts or new information, but from the fear that perhaps I had believed something false, or was living a lifestyle different from my true identity. The truth hadn't changed, and regardless of my emotions, the facts were still there, simply waiting for me to re-discover them.

I believe in questioning everything in search of the truth, but not primarily with *emotions* or other people's doubts and criticisms. Rather, I had to choose to use my own mind, reasoning and research.

I later realized that by letting doubts stress me, I was simply making my life harder. But when I gave myself a break from the *stress* of doubts, I experienced great relief. I still questioned things, but now I could question them objectively instead of just emotionally.

All my doubts came in different "phases," and still continue to come at times. But I find that I naturally come to a conclusion after a while, especially if I don't "freak out" or believe something automatically. And though one issue is usually replaced quickly by another, I learned to break the cycle of doubts dominating me.

I don't have an answer to everything in life, but *I can answer the negative attitudes* that try to take over my positivity. And it's like waking out of sleep to realize that previous days were just a series of doubts, not "the end of life as we know it."

Joplin, MO – May 22nd, 2011

Joplin's historic twister began its descent in Luke & Jana's neighborhood. This was what was left of their beautiful home.

But I believe this also pictures how we look when we allow others to affect us, or worse yet, from what we say and do to OURSELVES.

False Impressions

Rejection & Feelings of Worthlessness

"You are already an individual of value and potential. No one gave you those qualities, so no one can take them away."

A Different Kind of Pain

After moving away to college, I assumed I would have tons of new social opportunities. But friendships didn't just happen automatically. And when I didn't meet anyone to date right away, I became upset and bitter.

I think social pain can be one of the worst of all pains. How we make each other feel really can be more damaging than "sticks and stones." But perhaps rejection causes the worst damage of all. And sometimes the worst comes from those whom we thought were our best friends.

As things continued to not work out, I began to turn on myself. *"Perhaps something is wrong with me."* I began to punish myself on the inside. And while I had too much pride to cut my arms or slit my wrists, I was slicing my own soul without thinking twice.

It's a Personal Problem

In dating, my problem was always the fear of being rejected, which then led to inaction and actually *being* rejected. I was focused more on me and my fear than on the open opportunities right in front of me.

I then started trying to prepare myself psychologically for rejection, by assuming rejection *already.* This was supposed to give me early closure before I got hurt. But this also kept me from talking to people. I developed the habit of assuming the worst and asking questions *later.*

Even if I had gotten bad news, it would have been better to know the truth and get *closure* than to continue struggling for months on end. I had to learn to find something out for sure, so I could act on it, or move on with my life.

And in the few times that I was actually hurt by others, it would have helped so much to find out a little more about what they meant, calming myself down, and getting quicker resolution. Sometimes I had completely misunderstood anyway.

But even just assuming rejection caused unbelievable pain. I was damaging myself, including personal confidence. *I caused more pain to my own heart than most people ever did to me.*

I am big about second-guessing myself. And yes, it seems as if there's always more I could have done in a relationship. But then again, I tend to blame myself regarding social situations, though they are almost always more complicated than that.

Also, I found that some situations are going to go a certain way regardless of what I do. Those things in life just have to be accepted, like when two people realize they are not compatible, no matter how hard they try to make it work.

Clearly identifying the differences really helps me accept the loss, and has been one of the greatest things I've learned. And it applies to *many* negative situations.

Fitting In

Social pain for me was much broader than just romantic relationships. Most of the time I seemed to be the "odd one out" in a group, as if I didn't fit in.

I didn't feel "equal" with everyone else, especially when I didn't know what people were talking about in a conversation. It may seem silly, but this made me become harder on myself. I found myself abusing my self-image instead of protecting my personal perspective, personality and potential. Simply put, I began to quit believing in myself.

I've had to learn to accept social disappointments *while* keeping a sense of my own value. I found that it was not right to place my value on if a relationship works out, though I am very prone to do this. This was one of the greatest causes of my depression overall, and I usually have to combat these feelings at the *beginning.* Then I have to continue coming out of my shell to meet new people.

Freedom from Opinion

Remaining single made me feel like I must not be "good enough" for marriage, which led to even deeper thoughts of not having any value at all. I began to make the critical mistake of judging my own value based on the acceptance or rejection of others. This led to feeling worthless in society as a whole, and even in life itself.

And unfortunately, we sometimes allow people to hurt us more than they ever meant to. I had to realize that my value was NOT determined by how others make me feel.

But pain does not always involve what others do to us. I found that my pain can just as easily come from what I think about myself. And when I verbally say negative things about myself, it makes my negative self-image that much more established. **I believe that what we say about ourselves is just as important, maybe more, as what others say about us.** Each comment, if believed, has the power to damage us, or to build us up.

Pain and damage also came by what I *assumed* others were thinking about me, as if I was "saying it for them" in my mind. This began to cause the same hurtful feeling as if they had actually said cruel things to me.

I've had to commit to not allowing people's opinion of me, or what I *think* their opinion is, to change the good I already know about myself. **Other people do not determine *our* value!**

Value Added
"Perception" is everything, from the media in our lives, to our personal appearance, to peer-pressure. And playing in the back of our mind we sometimes hear the adage, "Only the strongest survive... "

From waiting on an acceptance letter, to getting a job, to watching what is featured on television, there are plenty of things to influence our definition of success. Unfortunately, we are tempted to measure our personal value by these things.

But does everyone fit into one definition of "strong" or "weak"? And who are the "weak," and is there no place in society for them? Do we get to determine *their* value? What if we find *ourselves* to be the weak ones, not matching up to someone else's definition of success? Would we look at things differently?

And yes, we can continue to try "climbing the ladder" of success, but I've also had to realize that not everyone climbs the same *ladder*.

And if we give up hope (feeling we have no potential or value), then we "fall off" the ladder we are on, and hit bottom, losing confidence in life.

So please don't fall into the trap I fell into, by trying to follow someone else's definition of success or failure. We all have value, including experiences and advice to share with others, as well as the time left in our lives to contribute in different ways. We are also still growing. *This is value added!*

One of the greatest things I did for myself was to LIST my personal values, even reminding myself of them daily, and updating the list. Why? Because it was so easy to forget who I am. I believe we need to keep our values in mind, because they are the **evidence** we need to face and defeat rejection and feelings of worthlessness.

Joplin, MO – May 22nd, 2011

TV did not tell half the story I witnessed while driving through Joplin for myself. I got lost looking for my aunt and uncle's house. Mile after mile of roads that I had walked before were now unrecognizable piles of former landmarks.

But this also pictures the depression that had been destroying my internal landmarks, turning personal values & qualities into a pile of debris. I lost sight of who I was.

Stealth Deceit

The Depths of Depression

"I've found that my depression only has power over me as long as I believe its message."

Where are You in the Journey?

The negative mental and emotional state I found myself in did not just happen overnight. The topic of each chapter in this book has been placed based on the natural progression of thoughts and feelings that led up to my depression.

And as you can see, the chapter titles in this book tell a story. Earlier insecurities led to anxieties, seclusion and loneliness. This led to doubt, then feelings of rejection and worthlessness. These ultimately opened the door to depression and even personal danger.

I am hoping anyone reading this will also check on where they might be in this progression, and seek a change before it is too late.

It has been like a roller coaster for me, experiencing the highs of success, then the lows of depressive thoughts about myself. But learning how to react to the lows has been critical for my surviving the ride.

Depression Does Not Discriminate

I never received "depression swimming lessons." I was going under, but not knowing how to respond. And it was not a one-time event, but became a regular occurrence.

Even "success" does not necessarily make us immune to depression. I had become very involved at Chattanooga State Community College, and loved every minute of it. From clubs, to retreats, to business meetings, to being elected student body president, to having the opportunity to meet the Governor of our state, I participated in practically everything.

My life now revolved around people and activities. And though the responsibilities could be stressful, I found purpose in everything, truly passionate about the tasks at hand. The support of the whole world was also around me, but it was no good to me, because I wasn't really using it.

I became better at hiding my struggles. And at college there were plenty of things to distract my mind, keeping me productive. Involvement became my escape. But until I *faced* my feelings directly, they would continue to wait on me, greeting me when I was alone or went home at night.

Especially since I was doing well in front of people, I didn't think I should talk about problems. I had the view that I needed to keep my struggles private, and just continue to compensate by being super-human-busy.

Gone Swimming

How does depression feel? I remember swimming one time at my grandparents' pond, wearing one of those ring floats around my waist. Of course as a child, I jumped into the air, and the preserver dropped to my ankles. I hit the water face first, heading straight for the bottom.

I can still see that green slime-water as I tried looking up to find the surface. I had even lost my orientation of which way was up. In that moment I actually tried screaming for help under the water. But I could only faintly hear myself, so I knew no one else could.

I remember seeing the ugly bottom of the pond as it rushed toward my face, but when it got there, reality struck. I saw that the bottom was actually my *friend*, something I could *push off of*. I came back to the surface easily.

When I make a mistake, or think I've offended someone, or see myself as aging out in life, I begin to sink again, seriously doubting life itself.

I can't really describe the depth of feelings that then takes me over practically at will, but the same drowning feeling returns. However, just like in my unofficial swimming lesson from the pond that day, there *is* a bottom to push off of.

The Storm Sets In

Back at college, I finally began to question what my depression was about in the first place. I realized it had taken me over without ever giving me any defined terms. I just felt worthless, and that I would never go anywhere in life. But why did it seem that my life *had* to end now? What was the proof, and WHY should I feel that way?

I found out that depressive thoughts *do not play fair!* They made me feel dysfunctional, but without even bothering to explain why. Don't let depression try to take you down without even having real reasons. Do some investigation!

At first it did seem that there was plenty of evidence. After all, was I really improving in life? I didn't feel like I was, even though the facts were to the contrary. I began to look at what I *wasn't* doing, and thinking I could never get there. Feelings had overtaken my better judgment. Negative thoughts not only attack our mind; they also attack our morale. Did you know that a lot of military warfare is actually fought psychologically? Morale can literally affect whole countries and economies, including the outcomes of wars or the stock market. How important then is our mindset, as we go about our daily life?

The Breakthrough

While sitting at a college concert, mesmerized by the talent on stage, I went through the lowest thoughts yet about myself. I looked back over my life, then imagining where I thought it would never be able to go. As tears began to fill my eyes now, the worst-yet state of depression set in. I really can't describe it. It was overwhelming.

All the negative feelings of the past converged in one moment. Depression told me that I had already reached my peak in life, and could go no further. I had also been a failure in love. I had reached a plateau in my job, and wasn't really capable of more. I didn't have all the things a person is supposed to have at my age, and there was nowhere to go now but down.

I didn't tell any counselors, even though they were right behind me at the concert... because "they might not understand." And there was nothing I could seemingly do either.

This is when it hit me that I was "trapped in my own mind." I will never forget when I mentally said those words to myself. I felt hopeless, but I had also finally defined my situation.

That is exactly when the first idea for this book-project came to me. I didn't know if people would understand, and I knew that if wrote my story, I'd be telling things I had not told *anyone* before, including my immediate family. But there had to be at least one person out there who also felt trapped on the inside. And if so, at least they might be able to relate and not feel entirely alone.

That's where a new journey started. This also gave me enough boldness to begin asking myself (really for the first time) *why* I was depressed. These things were very personal to me, and I thought that this book-project might hurt my identity or "image" in public. But I had to know, and if it took writing my story to figure things out, then I would.

However, instead of losing my identity, I FOUND an identity by being open and honest. It also led me to the path of overcoming and being able to relate to others.

But I had to call out each falsehood with the truth. And it was amazing how depression retreated into the corner when it was really exposed. This kind of depression only had power over me when I **believed** it! I had to *confront* the thoughts that were confronting me. Don't allow yourself to be lied to!

It's hard to have an effective answer (to depression) until we have a clear *question* (as to why we are depressed). And I began to find the things that my depression had built itself on.

I then had to take my depressive thoughts head-on. I began to list what personal traits or talents I could think of. And I thought of recent times that proved I was still growing. How then could future potential *not* be possible?

Surviving the Storm
There are many types of depression, and if struggles come down to needing a professional "diagnosis," then be *thankful* for this discovery, because now those things can actually be dealt with!

But I also believe in a type of depression that comes from negative thinking and emotional imbalance. We all have weaknesses, or somewhere we want to be in life, though not sure if we are good enough to get there. So when we fail, or things don't work out, we may feel like we are coming to the end of our self. We lose hope.

As my second-cousin Sara-Ruth told me one time, "What we think of ourselves can become a *self-fulfilling prophecy.*" The truth of this statement continues to grab me.

But my depression was also based on a false perception of myself. I didn't see this, however, until I tried to put my feelings into actual *words*. At first I couldn't do it. But then that bothered me too, because why couldn't I verbalize what was making me feel hopeless?

I began to call those thoughts out, so I could examine them. Eventually I began to see how ridiculous those false thoughts (of having no value) really were.

I began to "ask" my depression some pointed questions. For example, if I was feeling down after a social event, I would ask, "WHY is this making me feel invaluable? Had my expectations been too high?"

Then there was the matter of past failures. I had to tell myself that I knew I was sorry, that I had made things right, and that I had determined to grow and change for the future. Once I nailed these things down, negative thoughts couldn't get to me like before.

I later realized that my depression was actually communicating to me, exposing the things that really get to me. Instead of destroying me, it could serve as a means to growth!

The Lingering Storm

Another challenge came as I coped with depression. I found that I could *extend* or draw out my depression.

I have to watch out for certain influences in my life. For example, when I am driving down the road while listening to my favorite music, then everything is moving: my head, hands, feet, and yes, my mouth too, as I sing the lyrics (… hoping no one is looking as they drive by).

But certain songs or styles of music, however innocent, can also play on my attitude, triggering anger, sadness, or even depressive thoughts and feelings.

I have a few songs in my music database that I consider "the saddest songs ever." I don't want to give some of my music up. And many times performers have written lyrics out of their own personal struggles, which I relate to.

But I find that when I avoid certain songs or styles at least for a short time, especially when I am already down, I don't go as low. This also lets me get over my vulnerability, so I can listen with a different perspective.

I do not believe that influences and challenges in my life are actually the direct causes of depression. But the thoughts and emotional *reactions* that develop in me are what allow depression to take hold of me.

Please note that there are many other things which can tie into depression as well. But any time something is taking over my emotions practically at will, then I have to look into it, because something somewhere probably isn't right.

Steps to Ending the Storm

Sometimes thoughts were allowed to continue even *after* I had proven them wrong. I had gotten used to thinking low about myself, and now this was sneakily turning into a pity party. But why should we play the victim, when we can be the victor?

Just because a thought originated in my mind does NOT necessarily make it true. Finding what is false in depression and *seeing through* it can release us. "The truth will make you free."

But it's also been priceless to find someone who will *listen, understand,* and even *relate* (from their own struggles). A professional may be your greatest ally. And you don't have to be classified as crazy to simply receive helpful advice or an objective perspective.

Our challenges are usually more easily and accurately identifiable that we might imagine, because of countless others who, unknown to us, have faced the same things.

Also notice that depression does not offer a *solution* to the problems we are dealing with. Likewise, suicide doesn't actually fix problems either. It simply takes us out of the game. *And no game is won by forfeiting!*

I found that I really had to get to know myself. The closest person to me was *me!* I could already see my negative traits; they were underscored when I was depressed. But now I just had to turn that around and start seeing my positive qualities too.

What kind of qualities? Values which we are all born with, and which also have been acquired through experience and learning. Character, talent, education, and other things are just a few examples. And when I grow, I find that my future potential is also growing.

The big step for me was to take confidence in the value I had found in myself, and live by my strengths. Don't crawl into a corner like I did; grow and *invest* in your values.

Verbalizing the thoughts that get me down has been half the battle to overcoming them. The next step has been to *analyze* and see through them. Then I have to consistently *counter* them with the facts, until their power over me is broken.

Are you facing an ongoing struggle? Consider possible sources and responses:

Hormones/Physiological/Biological: Improve health with diet and exercise; be open to professional evaluation and treatment beyond what you can correct.

Childhood: Identify, see through, and break negative patterns.

Prior Situations: Go back as if in them again, addressing appropriately.

Social: Put positive people in your life; keep up with friends who can listen and relate. Start a "buddy" system of support.

Spiritual: Consider claiming the promises that come with faith.

Personal Thinking: Limit your over-reactions to life's circumstances. Develop positive patterns of thought; consider positive venting; get advice through a mentor or counselor.

Joplin, MO – May 22nd, 2011

It was hard to believe that I was looking at the former location of my second-cousins' home. The landscape looked completely different, and at first I even took a picture of the wrong house, thinking it was theirs. But no, this was their place now, after the storm - a bulldozed lot.

However, when it sunk in, this picture also reminded me of what I too would look like, if I let depression complete its work in me.

Ultimate Ending

Danger to Freedom

*"Ending my life was not fixing my problems.
It would simply end me,
creating problems for someone else."*

Water Skiing
I tried to balance as I put on water skis for the first time
ever. The boat was about to take off, and in those eternally
long seconds before the engine revved up, thoughts
flashed through my mind.

"What have I gotten in to?" "What if I make a fool of
myself in front of my friends?" "Will I even survive this
experience?"

I was up for a few seconds on that first ski run, then
overreacted to the waves, losing balance. I went under,
being dragged along. A few more attempts brought the
same results. Skiing seemed equivalent to "failing," and
some questions began to fill my mind...

*""Have I reached my max and will never do any better?"
"Can't someone else do this, and do it better?"
"Aren't there tons of other people with more ability than me?"
"Am I just becoming extra weight to people?"
"Is it worth it to fight again, only to fail again?"
"Don't repeated failures prove a larger point of failure?"
"Isn't the REAL failure actually ME?"*

These dark thoughts were some of the hardest for me to answer in life. I just couldn't see myself as having a place anymore. What if I was just pouring my life into a big hole? For a long time I had battled it out, but I was losing that battle. And I began to lose my will to survive.

Taking Off the Water Skis

Suicide was not just an emotional feeling for me. It involved an intellectual process which for sure did not happen all at once. It was actually something I said I would *never* do, or even consider. I didn't think I even had the guts to pull it off anyway.

But people change, and what I am about to say was not my plan for this book-project. But I feel I must include it. So here it goes...

Whether or not I realized it, I had begun to plan my end months before I actually gave up. I had selected a song that plays in the final death scene of a movie. The song was instrumental, but peaceful, in a sad way. It amplified how I felt. I played it over and over. I wanted to play it for others. I even recorded my own version of it.

About a year earlier my house had been robbed, and almost all my movies had been taken. But few had somehow survived, one of which was a children's movie. It was about a guy who had magical power, but was now coming to the end of his life. He said he was done, making room so that others could take his place. Those were the lines I wanted playing on my big-screen TV, in a repeating loop, when I passed away on my couch.

I also had a picture of myself from a few years earlier. I have no idea who took it, or exactly when, but it was of me waving goodbye, in a surreal sepia color (almost like a black and white photo). I had it positioned in my room, and I planned that later it would be out on my coffee table. This would be put with a note explaining my good intentions, but also my failure in life, and how I was saving the world from one more complicated person.

My goal was not to act out in violence, as others had done. There was no point in that, because that simply causes more problems in the world. And I wasn't frustrated with others. I was just frustrated with *me*, for not being able to handle myself, or the situations around me. So after a few final phone calls to express love and closure, I would simply pass away, silently, alone.

Why?

I actually had logical reasoning for why it was best for my life to be abbreviated. But as in higher arithmetic, theorems are only as good as the previous statements they are built on. This is true no matter how sound the logic that is being used. If the original statements are NOT correct, what are the chances that the conclusion will be accurate?

So it was with the logic I was using on my life. And when doubts and emotions had their way, all facts to the contrary were forgotten. I had to again pick up the proof of my value, and confront my doubts. But this was one of the hardest things to do, because I had stopped believing.

I knew that ending it all was not the way to go. But I just did not feel like making that next turn in the road. Ending everything was as simple as just letting the steering wheel stay where it was while I drove around a curve. I think it's amazing that I didn't even realize the hurt I would cause my family and friends by giving up and ending my life.

And what about my faith? It didn't matter, because I couldn't see God's promises really applying to me if I was a constant failure. After all, it was ME that was the failure... the one who would get upset at little things and cause hurts...the one who would just keep making the same mistakes again and again.

Answers
When I started this project, I had NO answers as to how I felt, or what I had been dealing with for so long. I just knew that my situation was getting more serious by the day. And it seemed better to turn my situation into a positive purpose for others, than to just continue down the path of danger that I was on.

I never saw myself as having a clinical condition, so I never sought diagnosis, or even professional advice. I hadn't even talked to a counselor, or tried to look at a book or website that could have helped, though I now wish I had. And while it turned out that I wasn't medically ill, my negative thoughts had practically *created* an illness for me.

But I was a fighter, and believed in fighting things alone. I truly wish I had at least sought counsel, before I let things progress.

Some challenges can be biological, hormonal, or simply bad luck in life. And I believe I had my share in all of those. But, regardless, the real struggle continued to be in my mind. And freedom came when I actually began to analyze what made me feel certain ways.

What were thoughts telling me exactly, that made life seem impossible to deal with? I had to literally take apart the ideas and feelings that were getting me down. Talking about or actually writing down these challenges gave me an outlet to what I was feeling.

It was as if I had stepped outside myself and could *objectively* see what I was dealing with. This completely changed my perspective on things, and I began to see *through* things, instead of those things being able to run freely through me.

The Team
I've discovered that issues not dealt with will hang on indefinitely, and can keep resurfacing. Others could have helped me to see my struggles objectively. But it's hard to have an objective opinion about your situation when YOU are the only one you listen to. Battles are easier won with a team, and sometimes ONLY won as a team.

Once I started talking, and others related, I felt completely different, and I discovered that victory was just around the corner. And if I had started by talking with a trusted family member or friend, (then a counselor or professional if needed), I believe I could have been freed much earlier.

However, my ultimate turning point was finally one day while driving and thinking about my story. Struggles had become practically constant now, even though I had just begun writing out my story.

All of a sudden, I realized the nature of what I had been thinking all these years. My depressive and hopeless thoughts could be summed up in one word: LIES! I had been lied to, not by others, but by negative thoughts and feelings about myself. Questions about seeing my value, believing in no potential, and even feeling trapped, were not realistic views of life.

These ideas were leading me to assumptions of having no real value, no future, and therefore *no hope*. But in one moment, the light went on. And though this feeling still returns, the power of this thinking was broken *immediately*.

This writing project took on a completely different approach. It became a discovery of myself, and of answers that worked for me. And yes, it also brought up many different struggles from my past. And as they resurfaced, I had to deal with some of them all over again. I have also found myself typing in tears, especially when I realized how far I had gone internally.

You may start thinking that it doesn't matter what happens to you. But I warn you that careless thinking *can* lead to careless action. You could be one step away from doing something that cannot be taken back. The reality of it is that when you feel at the end of yourself, this can be just as dangerous as really being in a physically dangerous situation.

Also, when we let helplessness, rejection and hopelessness (a DANGEROUS combination) turn into frustration and anger, then we may be putting ourselves and *others* at great risk. It is NOT necessary for struggles or depression to turn into anger, violence, or suicide. Rash reactions are NOT the way to make a statement or name for ourselves. *And they don't fix any problems.*

At a certain point I made a big decision: to actually take action regarding all these thoughts, and their emotions as well. Answers to my struggles seemed impossible to have, which is why I felt "trapped in my own mind." But something had to give.

This is why I cannot emphasize enough that we must also choose to note our past successes, and therefore our future potential. And when problems arise, I remind myself of those situations that have already worked themselves out. Wouldn't it be pre-mature for me to have quit because of them? So why quit now?

What I didn't expect was that by writing out my story, I actually would be *analyzing* it too. I began seeing through things that had plagued me for a number of years. Answers were *right in front of me*. I began to take things head-on. And at first it was a debate, but winning that debate now became feasible.

Describe, Discuss, Discover!
I can be stubborn, and I stuck to silence for over 15 years. I didn't realize the resources all around me that could have helped me make discoveries about myself.

Just as we are beings of physical, emotional, mental, and spiritual dimensions, so depressive feelings enter from these many perspectives (including our biological makeup, changing hormones, and even as a side effect to some medications, etc.).

But I also have noticed that for me, depressive feelings can be triggered by many things, such as circumstances, failures, guilt, rejection, or feeling worthless. It always helps me to **find the source** of what I am dealing with.

The process of describing how I feel, discussing it with someone who understands, and discovering the source of what I am dealing with, have been the critical keys to overcoming my challenges.

When my parents or friends tried to discuss things with me, I kept it all in. But I didn't realize how this was making my relationships difficult and even non-existent with others, as well as trapping my own self. I also did not realize the value of describing my innermost feelings and thoughts with someone.

Final Thoughts

I learned a unique perspective for when I am going through a situation that can trigger negativity. It helps me to place myself ten years in the future, "looking back" to see how *small* my present problems really are in the larger context. And this is a technique I continue to use. Do you see how this can completely change our way of looking at things?

Sometimes we can set too high of expectations for ourselves. But *know* that you *are* still growing, and that practically anything is possible to someone who is still adapting and developing new strengths in life. This puts the past behind us, and takes us into the future.

And yes, problems will still come, and we can always find areas to improve. The book of our lives is always being written. But even though it has many ups and downs in its chapters, at least we can know that each has a point and a lesson to learn. Our story of humanity truly can have a happy theme. And we CAN believe that our life's book will have a happy ending.

So I challenge you to write your own story! Don't allow life to just write your story for you. Know that *you* control your story! And it truly can have its own positive "twist," better than any novel, by turning negatives into positive answers. It is then that we don't ever have to look back.

Believe me, I know that insecurities and struggles can remain powerful and controlling even into adulthood. But when feelings say that we are weak, we have to counteract them by the truth, proving that we are not helpless or hopeless.

We can build on the confidence of prior successes, knowing that new stressful situations are also possible to deal with. I challenge you to describe your struggles, calling them out and addressing them appropriately. Also fall back on knowing that answers and resources are available. And most of all, *know that victory is yours for the taking.*

So let's join hands in *confronting* our challenges, not only for experiencing personal victory, but also for speaking up about the "silent threats" that are causing so many others to slip through the cracks.

Everyone has a story to tell. So let's raise awareness that there <u>is</u> an escape, that there <u>are</u> people who understand, and that WE **CAN** OVERCOME!

"Giving up on life will *take* **our identity, but overcoming in life will** *make* **our identity."**

What is Your Story?

We are all currently writing the story of our life.
But what will it say? Here are some ways we can begin
new chapters out of our current struggles.

Dig until you find the root.
Are there any past experiences, emotions or symptoms that may offer some understanding about current struggles? This also reveals our unique story to tell. Professional counsel may also be the key to helping with this.

Analyze until you find the progression.
Most likely serious challenges did not start all at once. Even medical situations seem to have a process to them. Looking back can give perspective; looking ahead can help in prevention. This is our continued story.

Take note of observations.
You might be surprised at the answers you discover for yourself. You may also be the key to helping someone else find their answers along the way!

Personal Evaluation

My first glimmer of hope came when I began asking questions about my struggles. And while hard to do at first, this allowed me to triage my situation and discover root causes.

Does it seem like low feelings just come out of nowhere? Could there be hereditary/physiological/clinical factors involved? Am I open to professional guidance/treatment as necessary?

Is there a link to past situations? Could I still be living within the realm of negative childhood memories or other experiences? Could my responses be based on learned behavior from the example of others (such as those who raised me)? Could my thoughts be used to trace deeper struggles/sources, such as a negative view of myself?

Are circumstances triggering certain emotional responses? What was happening when I started feeling low? Am I likely to overreact to certain situations? Was there something said or done that got me down? Are there any influences in my life that make me feel inadequate, worthless or hopeless?

Are my thoughts and emotions playing into my situation?
What was I thinking when I first started feeling low? Am I having any thoughts or feelings that I know are FALSE? Do any of my responses actually make the situation worse? Can I see personal patterns of negative thoughts or behavior that need to be changed? What works for me to make things better?

Does it seem like there is something bigger at hand? Does there seem to be a spiritual component that needs prayer? What support can I seek from friends? Are there professional services or counseling I can appropriately pursue?

Where "good" came out of "bad"...

I had the opportunity to visit my Uncle Phil & Aunt Barb's new home in Joplin (an upgrade made possible by Joplin's disastrous tornado).

With my surviving Great-Aunt Millie & Jana, in Joplin.

Jana & Luke's "Storm-Verse" of Testimony:

"For Thou hast been a strength to the poor, a strength to the needy in his distress, a refuge from the storm, a shadow from the heat, when the blast of the terrible ones is as a storm against the wall." Isaiah 25:4

The "Closet of Life." The hiding place that saved the lives of my second-cousins Jana & Luke during Joplin's massive tornado.

Speaking Out

Student-Stories

"SPEAKING OUT" has been written by students of Chattanooga State Community College. Each of them has dealt with and is overcoming their own set of diverse challenges.

I am daily encouraged by their "speaking out," and am so proud of the inspiration provided by their unique stories.

My Story

Topic: Surviving A Broken Relationship
(From a single mom)

I had a happy childhood. My parents were divorced... seems strange to say it was happy considering that... but, my mom remarried when I was two. My step dad was everything a dad was supposed to be and so much more. He was in the Navy and we moved around a lot. He pushed me to be well-rounded, to be everything I could be, the best me. My parents instilled in us the value of family, love, and support.

So when I was 17 and we found out he had cancer and only a few months to live, I was devastated. I threw myself into my schoolwork and spending time with my family while we were all still together. I had spent my life feeling like I had to be the best, to do the best. All I wanted was for my Dad to be proud of me, to see the sparkle in his eye when he introduced me to his co-workers. When he died the morning after my High School graduation, my journey with depression began.

I spent the next couple of years trying to figure out who I really was. How much had I done for his approval? To make him proud? For myself? I played softball, was a cheerleader, sang in the choir, was the class representative for student council, worked on the newspaper, yearbook, and was an artist. I had tried it all, but when my Dad died,

I felt like a huge piece of me died with him. I enrolled in school and was studying architecture. Then I met this guy. He wooed me and made me a million promises. I thought

I would be with him for the rest of my life. Everything seemed like it was finally coming together. I was going to be happy.

I quit school after my first year, and got a job working for the bank. But being married didn't seem to be quite what I had anticipated. I have to stop here for a moment and clarify, I really do believe in marriage. It's hard work and you have to work together to keep it strong, but when you do it's very rewarding and fulfilling. It was my relationship that wasn't working so well. I didn't realize how controlling he was until it was too late. Little by little every day I was slipping away, losing more and more of myself. I thought the answer was that we should have a baby. I could not have been more wrong; it didn't fix the relationship. While kids are a blessing in so many ways, they don't fix problems in any relationship.

From the outside looking in, we had the perfect family. A seemingly "happy" marriage, with two kids, a boy and a girl. We went to church, and he had a high paying job that allowed me to stay home with the kids. I volunteered at their school and at church. His high paying job kept him away from home a lot, 6 days a week until 7, 8 or 9 o'clock every night, and traveled 2-3 nights a week. When he did come home, he was still never really there. His phone, computer or the TV took precedence over us.

I felt invisible. I was going through the motions, feeling like a single mom. I did have friends, which he was extremely jealous over. He wanted the same relationship with me that I had with them, but he didn't want to put the time and effort into the relationship. He managed to convince me that they were using me and taking advantage of me - whatever it took for me to cut them out of my life and think it was all my idea. I ended up on anti-depressants so I could get through the day, so I could stop crying, so I wasn't curled up in a ball in the bed. I had never felt so alone.

I reconnected with my best friend that I had known for 20 years. He reminded me of who I used to be. I remember one of the first things he said to me was "What happened to you? Where did you go?" The more I talked to him, the more I realized how lost I really was. As I started to put back the pieces up one by one, something happened... I started to feel happy again. I felt like getting out of the bed, putting on real clothes instead of pajamas, fixing my hair, putting on makeup, keeping the house clean, working out. But, all the happiness came with a price. I was accused of having an affair, and it was the perfect excuse for my husband to leave.

The first counseling session I went to with my Pastor, my kids told the entire staff at church, "My Mom and Dad are getting divorced!" At first I was appalled, shocked and terrified of "What will everyone think of me now?" But, what I found is people are very loving! People want to love on you, they want to help you, they want to support you, they want to encourage you, they want to be there for you when you need a shoulder to cry on! You can't get that support if you never say anything, if you feel too ashamed, too full of pride to admit you're struggling and you need help. God places people in your life for very specific reasons; it's no accident they're there.

Through my journey I realized a butterfly is the result of painful change. You impact everything around you; the world is more than what happens to you. I let my insecurities take over and other people's opinion validate me and my feelings. I turned it all over to God and he gave me 8 verses to carry me through.

> *"For I know the thoughts that I think toward you, saith the LORD, thoughts of peace, and not of evil, to give you an expected end."*
> *Jeremiah 29:11*

"Brethren, I count not myself to have apprehended: but this one thing I do, forgetting those things which are behind, and reaching forth unto those things which are before, I press toward the mark for the prize of the high calling of God in Christ Jesus."

Philippians 3:13-14

"Rest in the LORD, and wait patiently for him: fret not thyself because of him who prospereth in his way, because of the man who bringeth wicked devices to pass."

Psalm 37:7

"It is of the LORD's mercies that we are not consumed, because his compassions fail not. They are new every morning: great is thy faithfulness. The LORD is my portion, saith my soul; therefore will I hope in him."

Lamentations 3:22-24

"Grant thee according to thine own heart, and fulfill all thy counsel."

Psalm 20:4

"Create in me a clean heart, O God; and renew a right spirit within me. Cast me not away from thy presence; and take not thy holy spirit from me."

Psalm 51:10-11

"But they that wait upon the LORD shall renew their strength; they shall mount up with wings as eagles; they shall run, and not be weary; and they shall walk, and not faint."

Isaiah 40:31

"Have not I commanded thee? Be strong and of a good courage; be not afraid, neither be thou dismayed: for the LORD thy God is with thee whithersoever thou goest."

Joshua 1:9

This journey has been hard! It's challenged me, it's broke me, it's strengthened me, it's fulfilled me. I wouldn't change any part of it. I couldn't be half of what I am today, if even one small part had been different. I know how scary it is, but God will get you through.

What do you want from your life? It's a long hard road to figure that out and to take the steps to get there, but it's worth every second. Truth is, your world's not caving in on you! It's just your perspective on it.

My design teacher once said "When you think you have it just the way you want it, turn it upside down and look at it from a different viewpoint. Then you can see what's missing!" You can get through it; don't shut down, don't shut people out, reach out to someone; there's a hand waiting for you!"

My Personal War

The Secret Reality of Substance Abuse
(From a student-leader)

If you're going to do it, just do it at home", my mother said at the beginning of my 14th summer. That phrase was the beginning of a long, long love affair with drugs. Pot is first, last and foremost in the many substances that I have tried, and honestly still haunts me to this day.

Now don't think that I'm blaming my using on my mother, but some background into my history is still relevant. I am the oldest of 3 that I grew up with (I have 5 brothers and sisters) by six years. My grandfather and stepfather were both alcoholics. We moved around a lot, once in my 6th grade year because my house burned to the ground, and a year later my mother left my stepfather and moved us back to Ft. Oglethorpe, GA. We were always poor, living in areas that most people don't like to drive through at night.

So at 16 I started working full time and dropped out of school. Now I did have friends, (move as much as I did and you learn how to make them fast) and the easiest friends to make are the ones who want to get messed up with you. So after dropping out and having plenty of free time, life became one giant party. Weed, booze, and acid became regular friends of mine, always around waiting for me to have some fun.

This went on for several years, until I tried to stop smoking weed and found cocaine and pain pills. My girlfriend at the time bet me that I couldn't stop smoking weed for 6 months and my naturally competitive self bet that I could. And I did, by replacing it with harder drugs.

Getting drugs is easy. Somebody is always around that can help you find what you need. My "salvation" during this bet was a guy at work. We had talked a few times and if someone has the right look then the subject is going to come up. So I started buying coke from him to "get me through the night". Now this whole time I'm still binge drinking and taking pain pills that I buy from another "friend". So in the end I won the bet but lost the war, because now I had a taste for stimulants and pain killers.

After that it was on and I did everything that didn't involve a needle. Eventually all this would slowly start to fade away, but only after some really bad events over a few years did I get this problem back to just weed and booze.

I know this story would be great if it had a happy ending, but sadly it doesn't. I still fight every day to try and stay sober. I probably need to get some help, learn some skills to help me cope and say no to the urge. But taking the first step toward recovery is always the hardest. The stigma associated with drug abuse is huge, and the shame of not being strong enough to quit is immense.

How do you ask someone to trust you or take you seriously when the word addict is hanging over your head? I know that there is no quick fix to my problem, and also know that anytime the stress builds up I will be tempted again.

It becomes a vicious cycle of not being able to cope, using, being even more unable to cope, using again over and over and over. Being stressed isn't the only reason anyone, including me, gets high, so don't take that statement as an excuse. You get high because it's fun and you enjoy it.

Pretty soon you start to feel like the only time you can have any fun is if you're high while you do it. This all goes on and on until you hit a wall and think you need to change. And you may make that change, get on the wagon and stay there, but that drive is still going to haunt you. It is not a switch that can just be turned off, but a battle you fight every day of your life with every aspect of your being.

It's A Gift

Dealing with Diagnosis
(From a now-successful business woman)

I was diagnosed at 15 with PTSD (post-traumatic stress disorder) and medicated (Geodon, Valium, Adderrall, to name a few; over time, over 25 medications).

Throughout high school, I saw many psychiatrists and counselors. I don't know how much this helped me, because I was still depressed, and bad things kept happening to me. But I think it's extremely important for people to be diagnosed and treated professionally, because who knows if I would have been worse without it.

Luckily, in college I was finally diagnosed as bi-polar, with schizo and psychotic affect. That means that when I have a manic episode, I also experience the symptoms of hearing voices and having hallucinations and delusions.

I consider this state of mind a gift, now that I've come to know it ten years later. But through the course of getting to know myself and my relationship to my illness, I've been hospitalized four times, meaning my symptoms grew so strong that I couldn't function in regular society. I didn't have both feet on the ground. I was unaware that humankind was continuing on without me.

But I value those experiences because I learned a lot about myself and how my brain works. I can use what other people call mental illness, not as an illness, but as a part of who I am, as long as I know how to control it.

The biggest thing I have learned is that if I live my life comparing myself to others, or imagining that others are judging me, then I will be in a constant state of anxiety. I have had to learn to eliminate fear and self -doubt, and the notion that what I have is a disease. Every person on this planet is unique and special, and has something to offer the world.

And I have had to learn the hard way that not everybody feels that way (unfortunately there are mean people in this world). But, I don't have to associate with those people. The fastest path to happiness is learning to accept who I am, gifts, flaws and all; and learning to love that person in the here and now, as I am today. Not who I may be, or who I was, but who I am.

On this path, this journey of life, it is essential to have mentors, teachers, spiritual guides, and counselors that you can trust. But also having a professional psychologist and psychiatrist, who has made it their study to learn about the brain and how it works, is imperative. As you go through life, there has to be someone that you can tell everything to, and that you can be completely honest with. Especially the negative stuff, because if we keep it inside, it will destroy us.

A talk-therapist is trained to understand the human condition, and all the various aspects of it. But don't let yourself be fooled; if you feel any distrust or weirdness, any discomfort at all with your therapist, don't feel that you must keep them. YOU are the one in charge. They must be someone you feel comfortable with, and that has the same values as you. Find someone who treats you with respect, not as a patient with an illness to be fixed, but as a person.

The importance of talking out my life situations, from the minutia details to the big events that formed who I am, can't be overstated. The combination of medication and a trusted counselor saved my life. There's no pill to make you a different person, or to take away your past. But talking to someone about your life and the events that matter to you is invaluable.

A Story from the West Side

From the Streets to Success
(From a student leader and graduate)

I grew up in the projects, where we stayed until I was 13. Being a teenager coming of age, I had problems where I didn't talk, where I was in a shell. I had ideas to express, but I didn't know how to get them out. My mother and stepfather were young themselves, and didn't know how to talk to me, or ask the right questions, to pull the answers out of me. So it was like a ball of energy over here, and a ball of energy over there.

When my mother graduated from community college she married my stepfather. But he beat her and abused me and my sisters. So my escape was to leave and continuously stay with my grandmother. I never had a father around. In my mind I felt like I didn't have anybody.

I didn't meet my real father until I was 13. He got out of jail and stayed with me for about a week, and then moved to Atlanta. Previously, I felt that he was like an escape, like a door that I had never seen, that I could go to and open up. Now for the first time in my life I felt complete, after seeing him that one time. But after he moved I got a phone call saying that my father had been murdered by an old girlfriend who visited him and stabbed him in the chest when he answered the door.

I went to the streets and started 'gang-banging.' One of the major reasons I joined the gang was that I met other people who were just like me. And the pain and problems we were going through made us bond even closer. They became my family, my mother and father, brothers and sisters, and taught me just like you would teach your son or daughter, except in negative aspects.

But the only thing that separated me from them was the fact that my grandmother gave me God at a young age. Instead of reading bedtime stories, she read Bible stories like Jonah and the Whale. So whenever I would go out there and do wrong to be accepted in the gang, the God that she instilled in me brought me back to reality. Every time I got way out there past myself, I had the feeling that it was wrong.

The major thing you were taught in the streets was that you don't have feelings. And if you do have feelings, then you're weak, and the weak are the ones who get killed. So I grew up bottling all these feelings that I had, about missing my father, missing my grandmother, and not knowing how to talk to the person who brought me into this world. So it was just like being an adult, but without the responsibilities or the respect of being an adult.

As I got older, I started taking those feelings of not having a mother, to the different females that were in my life. The streets taught me to go around and get every woman you can get.

So at 18 or 19 years of age, I started going out. And whatever problem you had, as long as you had five or six girls, you were king. That defined your manhood. And if you had a nice car, or nice clothes, that defined your manhood. It was nothing about where you worked, or how you got your money, or how you treated people around you. Because in the streets it was either kill or be killed.

So I got my own makeshift family, and got jobs like doing dishes to make my wife happy. The streets taught me that if you keep a "grocery list" of things to do, like to pay the bills, and to be with your wife, and to tend to the kids, then that's all there is to being a husband. But when it came to situations, I didn't know how love, or how to let my feelings out. Love is not on that list. The pretense of love is there, but not love itself. The list that God gives us is patience, kindness, not envying, not boasting, and not self-seeking. I didn't know any of those things. It was the opposite of what I had been trained to do.

What do you do when you have so much depression, so much anger, that you can't bottle it up? It manifested itself in everyday things. When I was driving down the street, I would start crying. When I was with friends, I would bring the whole mood down. But because I had a reputation on the streets, everybody around me was scared to say anything. When I came home, my kids would run away from me, which was really hurtful. They related me to being a disciplinarian. "Daddy's mad all the time."

I was dealing with anger in a way that I didn't know I was dealing with it. I wanted love, but I didn't know at that time what love was. I did all the things on that list, but my wife still went out and found somebody else. And when I asked her about it, she said it was because they told her she was pretty. But you see, that wasn't on the list! She said other guys sat down and talked to her, and took the time out to get to know her. But those weren't on the list either!

I had two extremes: either I was extremely happy about everything, or I was extremely mad. I didn't know how to be in between, and I didn't know how to respond to problems when they came around me. I loved my wife so much, but when she started going out and seeing other men, I went back to my traditional ways of top notch anger. And when I caught her doing that, I got with the guy, beat him up, and almost killed a guy.

Around this time the O. J. Simpson trial came out. And when police were called to a house, regardless of the argument, someone was going to jail. And my wife at the time was much smaller, so when I stood up, being so big, I was going to jail. And my wife understood this and was devious too, so I ended up doing six months.
But I believe jail saved my life. Jail is where I learned how to love.

There was an older gentleman in there that was always sitting in the corner, reading in the Bible, or telling someone else about it. I hated this man, and did not want anything to do with him. I thought he was the corniest man out there, and if he said anything to me, I was going to knock his block off.

One day in jail I was hungry, and didn't have anything. I asked a friend for food, but they said no, because I didn't have any money on the books. This old gentleman heard me, and put two oatmeal cakes on the bed. But that's something no one does in jail, unless they want something in return. So I was fuming, and went over there to "check him," to do some harm to him, because that's like someone spitting in your face.

I was standing in his face, because I was about to make an example out of him before he made an example out of me. But he said that he didn't mean to disrespect me, and that I could go ahead and beat him up, but that it was not anything like that. It was at that moment in time that the God that my grandmother had instilled me, gave me peace, and calmed me down.

So we sat down and started talking, and he asked me what I was in for. But in jail that's not something you talk about, because they could go and snitch on you and get your time increased, and theirs decreased. But I felt so at ease with him that I told him what I was in for, and he started telling me, "How can you be a man if you don't know how to be a man? You need someone to teach you." He started telling me about 1 Cor.13:4-8, and I applied that to my heart.

After I got out of jail and knew what love was, I started wrestling with my inner self, with the new me and the old me. Is it weak for me to go and seek professional help? Is it weak for me to even say I had a problem? You see, that was not something talked about in my culture or community. Who do you talk to? I couldn't go to my family, because they only talked about slavery, and were taught to internalize all this hurt, anger and pain. So if you wanted to actually go out there a talk to someone, you were weak. "Only white people talk to counselors." It's easy to go out there and get into trouble. That's a natural thing. But for me to do right, I had no one around me to teach me these things.

But I remembered my grandmother taught me that God puts people in our life for a time and season. So I had to do something unconventional. I went out and sought the help of a psychiatrist. I realized I did have a problem with anger, confrontation, and communication. I had limitations, but since I didn't talk about them, I didn't know what they were until I talked to a psychiatrist. They helped me with those issues.

They showed me that when I'm getting angry in a conversation, it's ok to walk away and continue it later on. It's ok to go out there and find a punching bag when you find your anger limits being reached. Or do something creative with it. Anger can be a positive thing too. When you're out there working and you get angry, work HARDER! Try to think of ways to get through it, instead of using anger as a destructive tool.

I got depressed too. Because after dealing with all those feelings over the years, it was too much for me to put inside this bottle, to lock them up inside my heart. So I wanted the relief. It was an everyday agonizing pain. It was a role to me after a while, like being in the greatest play that I could ever play; I was playing 'me' and I just got tired of doing it. I was trying to seek and find a way to relieve all this agonizing pain.

It was like a thousand knife pricks every single day. Every time I thought about my father, a feeling of excitement came over me, then knowing he wasn't there overcame that feeling, and made the sadness even worse. And consequently every person that I really cared about ended up leaving my life, and I equated that with me doing things wrong. And I didn't know how to talk to anyone, or where.

Twice I tried to commit suicide (I drunk poison initially, then took pills). Each time when I felt myself about to black out and going beyond myself, I called out for help. So looking back, that lets me know that I didn't want to commit suicide; I wanted to stop the pain.

These things happened in my early twenties. I am 38 years old now, and the same feelings I had then I have now. But one of my tools is to go and talk to people about it, and not be ashamed. You don't necessarily have to tell people that you are depressed and about to commit suicide. I truly believe that once you've tried to commit suicide you will always think of it as much easier to try the next time. So now I find ways to battle those thoughts. And when I want to take the easy way out, I think of my kids. I think of the people around me, and how that would affect them in some way.

And I see people now expect God to stop things with His finger "just like that," but He puts people in our lives to help us with that anger. And it takes time to stop being depressed, and to find out who you are. Nobody knows you like you. You can feel when you've reached your limitations, and it's your responsibility to get up and do something about it. You may not be able to say your exact feelings, but maybe you can say close to it.

I learned over time that it was okay to discuss it, because other people understood. You can't trust everybody with your feelings, because they can use them to your advantage. It's up to me to find that person in my life that I can trust, black or white, red or blue.

No one wants to have face to face interaction, because we're afraid of what people may say to us, or the expression on someone's face. I was scared of the question of why I was dealing with things, and how people would view me. Because everybody tells you 'don't be sad; don't be angry.' And they expect all that to be over just because they said it.

Anger is a part of life. Depression is a part of life. You can't just cut feelings off, because eventually you will still get depressed. And if you don't respect your feelings, your feelings will make you respect them.

But if I could say one thing, the key to it is talking. Open up enough where you can talk. Respect your feelings. Brushing it off is no good for anybody. You hurt for a reason. Understand what that reason is, and deal with it. Have someone to help you deal with it.

And if I hadn't gone through the things in my life, I probably wouldn't be sitting right here. I would be dead. I've looked down the barrel of a gun and seen the fire come out, holding my oldest son in my hands, and wondering where the bullet went.

Believe it or not, the same thing that was applying 1,000 pounds of pressure on me is the same thing that leaves me here; that is, dealing with depression. Because in my community talking to people and saying you are depressed is an unheard-of thing.

So if there is a need for someone to come out and speak on their behalf, then I will. I don't care if I have to be the first one. Because if someone is having the same problems and feelings that I have, and it stops them from hurting themselves, then maybe that's why I went through those things. Someone had to teach me. So I am still here, and I know I am here for a reason. I hope some of this helps you."

Write Your Own Story!

Have you ever considered telling your story? Here's some tips:

Consider the motivation for telling your story (such as desiring to make personal discoveries/helping others through the details of your experiences). But also note that it may be *very* hard to start writing at first, especially while feeling low.

Consider venting by writing when you feel lowest, but also writing during the positive times. That's when I feel more confident to share, as well as being able to take a more <u>objective</u> look at what I'm dealing with.

Start by just making a few notes. I started with a short-list of observations about my own situation. A few questions that I started asking myself were: *What am I dealing with, that I can start identifying (past experiences, patterns of emotion, specific thoughts, etc.)? What observations have I made, such as links between my feelings and the past, and whatever may be causing them? What works for me to make things better?*

Take steps to become open and a resource for others. I was the *last* person wanting to share my innermost struggles. But the writing process helped me heal, get closure, and overcome. It ALSO gave me a reason to talk with others (*"I'm starting a writing project. It's my story. What do you think of this topic?"*) The responses & stories similar to my own blew me away.

Just tell your story. It wasn't easy, but I finally let out the details. I went all the way back to my childhood, tracing the history of each challenge I was facing. And when I laid it all out, a pattern became visible, of how one experience and emotion had led to another. I was able to chart my past, AND a new direction for my life.

Other Reading

Some friends shared a number of books with me as I finished *Trapped in My Own Mind*. Here are a few that surprised me with points which related to my own challenges.

Seamands, David A. *Healing for Damaged Emotions: Recovering from the Memories That Cause Our Pain*. Colorado Springs: Chariot Victor, 1991.

Meier, M.D., Paul. *Blue Genes, Breaking Free from the Chemical Imbalances That Affect Your Moods, Your Mind, Your Life, and Your Loved Ones*. N.p.: Tyndale's House, 2005.

Minirth, M.D., Frank, and Paul Meier, M.D. *Happiness Is a Choice, The Symptoms, Causes, and Cures of Depression*. Updated ed. Grand Rapids: Baker, 2007.

Carter, M.D., Les, and Frank B. Minirth, M.D. *The Freedom from Depression Workbook*. Nashville: Thomas Nelson, 1995.

Contact Us

Do you have a personal story or resource that has helped you? Please don't hesitate to contact us!

Join us on Facebook:
"Not Trapped Anymore!"

Or email us:
onthecuttingedgetv@gmail.com

Twitter: "OTCuttingEdgeTV"
(Get Regular Updates)

YouTube Channel: "OnTheCuttingEdgeTV"
(Watch Our Related Video Series Online)

Blog: http://nottrappedanymore.blogspot.com
(Check Out Thought-Provoking Posts)

Helplines

National Hopeline Network
1-800-SUICIDE (784-2433)
www.hopeline.com

National Eating Disorders Association
1-800-931-2237
www.nationaleatingdisorders.org

S.A.F.E. Alternatives (Self Abuse Finally Ends)
1-800-DONTCUT (366-8288)
www.selfinjury.com

The Hopeline
1-800-394-HOPE (4673)
www.thehopeline.com

Support & Counseling Services
Online International Locator
www.befrienders.org

Abuse Hotline Numbers
1-800-799-SAFE (7233)
www.stopfamilyviolence.org

CPSIA information can be obtained at www.ICGtesting.com
Printed in the USA
LVOW12s0342091213

364383LV00005B/120/P